W9-DHG-829

DISCARD

CRAFTS FOR ALL SEASONS

CREATING
COSTUMES

Important Note to Children, Parents, and Teachers
Recommended for children ages 9 and up.
Some projects in this book require cutting, painting, gluing, and the use of small materials. Young children should be supervised by an adult. Due to differing conditions, individual levels of skill, and varying tools, the publisher cannot be responsible for any injuries, losses, or other damages that may result from use of the information in this book.

Published by Blackbirch Press, Inc.
260 Amity Road
Woodbridge, CT 06525

©2000 by Blackbirch Press, Inc.
First Edition

Originally published as: *Disfruta Haciendo Disfraces* by Roser Piñol, Professor of Art.

Original Copyright: ©1995 Parramón Ediciones, S.A., World Rights, Published by Parramón Ediciones, S.A., Barcelona, Spain.

e-mail: staff@blackbirch.com
Web site: www.blackbirch.com

Printed in Spain

10 9 8 7 6 5 4 3 2 1

Library of Congress Cataloging-in-Publication Data
Piñol, Roser.
[Disfruta haciendo disfraces. English]
Creating costumes / by Roser Piñol.
    p.   cm. — (Crafts for all seasons)
Includes index.
Summary: Describes how to make many costumes and accessories out of everyday materials.
ISBN 1-56711-438-5 (hardcover : alk. paper)
1. Costume—Juvenile literature. 2. Masks—Juvenile literature.
3. Handicraft—Juvenile literature. [1. Costume. 2. Handicraft.]
I. Title. II. Crafts for all seasons (Woodbridge, Conn.)
TT633 .P56 2000   00-008070
745.54'2—dc21   CIP
                                                                  AC

Contents

✄ = *Adult supervision strongly recommended*

BLACK

CRAFTS FOR ALL SEASONS

CREATING
COSTUMES

BLACKBIRCH PRESS, INC.
WOODBRIDGE, CONNECTICUT

Vibrant Visors

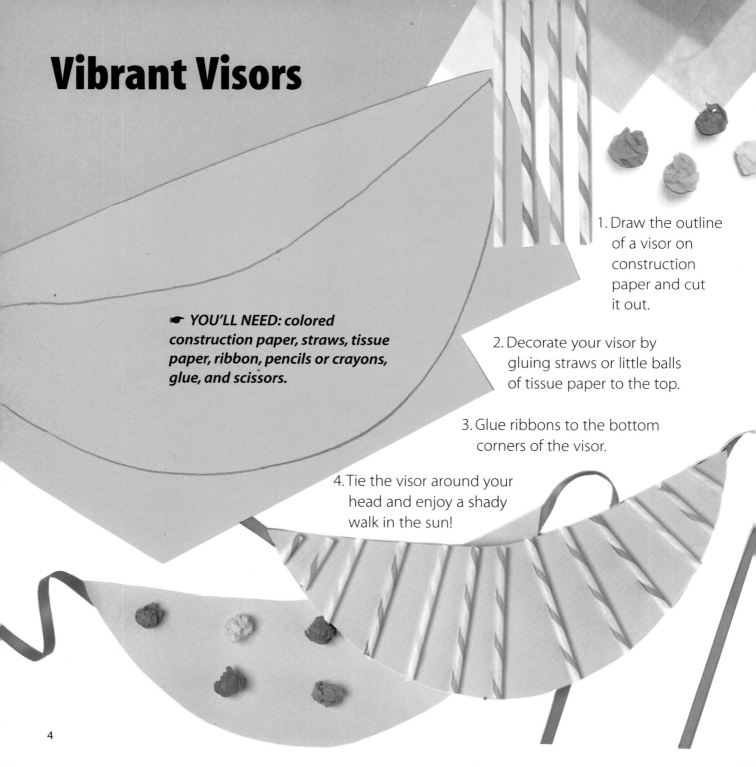

☛ YOU'LL NEED: colored construction paper, straws, tissue paper, ribbon, pencils or crayons, glue, and scissors.

1. Draw the outline of a visor on construction paper and cut it out.

2. Decorate your visor by gluing straws or little balls of tissue paper to the top.

3. Glue ribbons to the bottom corners of the visor.

4. Tie the visor around your head and enjoy a shady walk in the sun!

Peter Pan Hat

☞ YOU'LL NEED:
construction paper,
glue, and scissors.

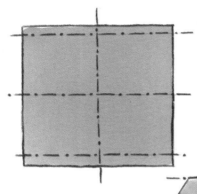

1. Take a square
   sheet of paper
   and fold it as
   shown.

💡 *Use your imagination:*
Make a festive party hat.
Decorate your hat to
fit an upcoming
holiday!

2. Make a feather by cutting
   an oval shape. Cut small slits
   for a fringe on both sides.

3. Cut out a strip to decorate
   the hat.

4. Glue the
   feather
   and the
   strip to
   the hat.

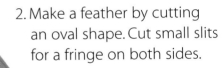

5

Royal Crowns

☛ **YOU'LL NEED: typing paper, posterboard, construction paper, gold paper, colored ribbon, stickers, glue, and scissors.**

1. Fold a strip of gold paper accordion-style. Draw the outline of a crown on one edge of the folded strip and cut it out.

2. Unfold the strip and trace its shape on the back of a sheet of posterboard.

3. Glue the gold crown to the cardboard and cut it out. Then glue a strip of ribbon to the crown.

4. Add "precious stones" to your crown by using stickers or gluing on paper cutouts.

5. Roll up the crown and glue the ends together. Now take charge of your realm!

💡 *Use your imagination:*
Cut different shapes and designs into the top of your hat for more fun!

A Showy Shawl

● *YOU'LL NEED:*
crepe paper, tissue paper,
colored paper, glue, ribbon,
and scissors.

1. Cut a strip of fringe from tissue paper.

2. Cut a triangle out of crepe paper.

3. To hide the border between the fringe and the shawl, glue a ribbon to the edge of the fringe before you glue it to the shawl.

4. Cut petals and circles out of colored papers.

5. Glue the petals to the circles to create different-colored flowers.

6. Now show off your shawl on your shoulders!

💡 *Use your imagination:* *You can use the same techniques to create bandanas or even flags!*

Perfect Party Hats

☛ **YOU'LL NEED: colored construction paper, tissue paper, crepe paper, an elastic band, glue, and scissors.**

1. Cut two triangle-shaped pieces out of construction paper.

2. For a clown hat, use strips of tissue to make paper balls, as shown.

3. For a sultan's hat, cut off the tip of the triangle.

4. Make a rope with two strips of crepe paper by twisting them together.

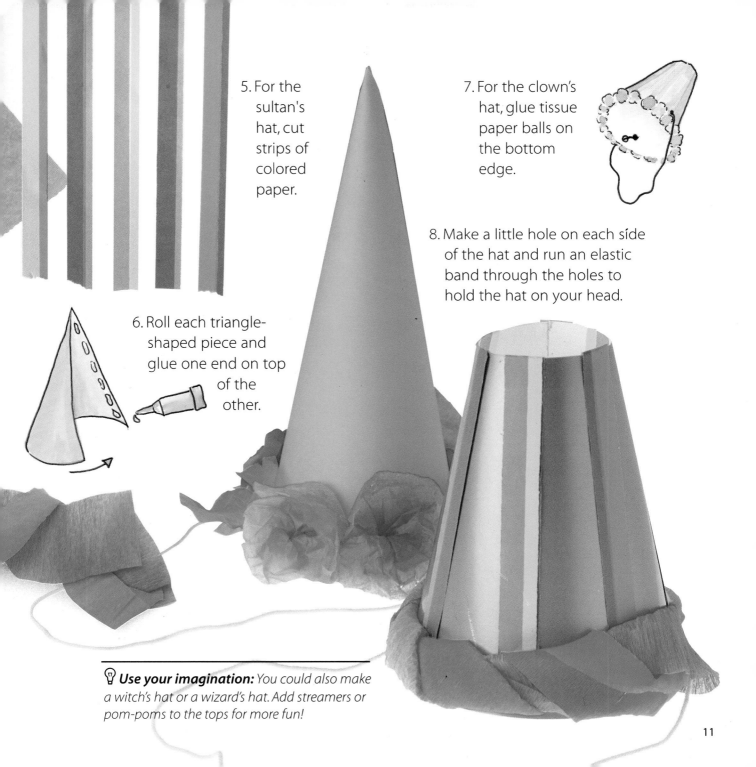

5. For the sultan's hat, cut strips of colored paper.

6. Roll each triangle-shaped piece and glue one end on top of the other.

7. For the clown's hat, glue tissue paper balls on the bottom edge.

8. Make a little hole on each side of the hat and run an elastic band through the holes to hold the hat on your head.

💡 **Use your imagination:** *You could also make a witch's hat or a wizard's hat. Add streamers or pom-poms to the tops for more fun!*

Wacky Waitress Outfit

☞ YOU'LL NEED:
construction paper, ribbon, cloth, paper doilies, a marker, scissors, and glue.

1. Take a paper doily and roll a ribbon halfway onto the doily, as shown.

2. To make the apron, cut a half-oval shape out of white construction paper.

3. Cut two pockets out of a piece of cloth.

4. Make top flaps out of colored doilies or construction paper.

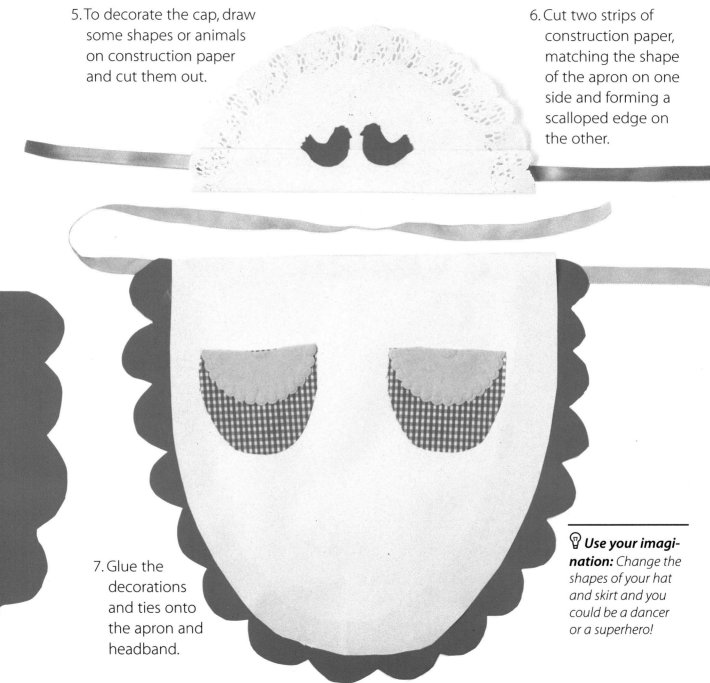

5. To decorate the cap, draw some shapes or animals on construction paper and cut them out.

6. Cut two strips of construction paper, matching the shape of the apron on one side and forming a scalloped edge on the other.

7. Glue the decorations and ties onto the apron and headband.

💡 **Use your imagination:** *Change the shapes of your hat and skirt and you could be a dancer or a superhero!*

Flower-Power Headbands ✂

☞ **YOU'LL NEED: different-colored construction paper, a paper hole punch, crepe paper, a marker, ribbon, glue, and scissors.**

1. Cut a strip of construction paper for a headband. Ask an adult to make holes in it, as shown.

2. Cut a rectangle of colored crepe paper for each flower.

3. Fold the crepe paper strips accordion-style.

4. Run a ribbon through a pair of holes.

5. Use the ribbon to attach a flower to the construction paper strip.

6. Open the folded strips to make flowers.

14

7. Ask an adult to help you curl the ends of each ribbon with scissors.

8. Do the same for each flower.

9. Once you've placed all the flowers, glue or tie the two ends of your headband together. Now your headband is ready to wear!

💡 **Use your imagination:** *Decorate your headband with circles and gems for a royal tiara, or use seashells for a mermaid's headband!*

15

Costume Ball Masks ✂

☞ YOU'LL NEED: construction paper, glue, glitter, a pencil, a rubber band, ribbon, a plastic straw, transparent tape, and scissors.

1. Draw half of your mask on a folded sheet of paper and cut it out. This will be the pattern.

2. Use the pattern to trace the design on a sheet of construction paper.

3. Cut out the mask.

4. Decorate it with glitter, starting at the edges. Add sequins or paper designs if you like! Do horizontal strips and antennae for a bee mask.

5. Attach a rubber band or ribbon to either end for tying to your head. If you like, you could tape or glue a plastic straw to one side and hold your mask to your face.

💡 *Use your imagination:* *Try cutting eye holes in different shapes, such as diamonds, rectangles, or even stars!*

Happy Hula Outfit

1. Cut a strip of construction paper that fits around your waist.

2. Cut strips of different colors of tissue paper.

3. Glue the tissue paper strips to the back of the construction paper strip.

☛ **YOU'LL NEED:**
colored construction paper, colored tissue paper, a pencil, glue, and scissors.

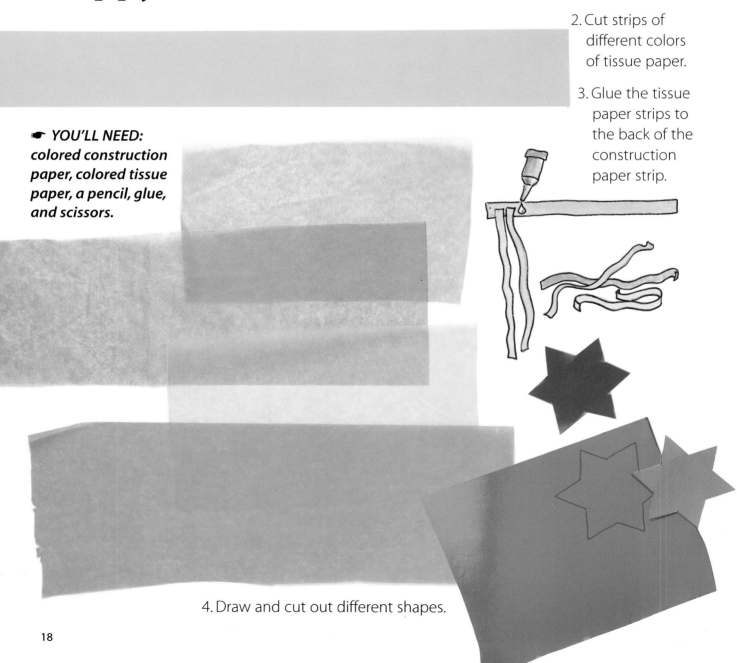

4. Draw and cut out different shapes.

5. Cut a strip of fringe out of tissue paper.

6. Glue the fringe to the paper strip and ruffle it.

7. Finish decorating the skirt by gluing on the shapes.

8. You can make a lei necklace the same way. Now you're ready to hula at a luau!

💡 *Use your imagination:* *Try decorating your hula skirt and lei with flowers made from small balls of tissue paper.*

Nifty Necklaces

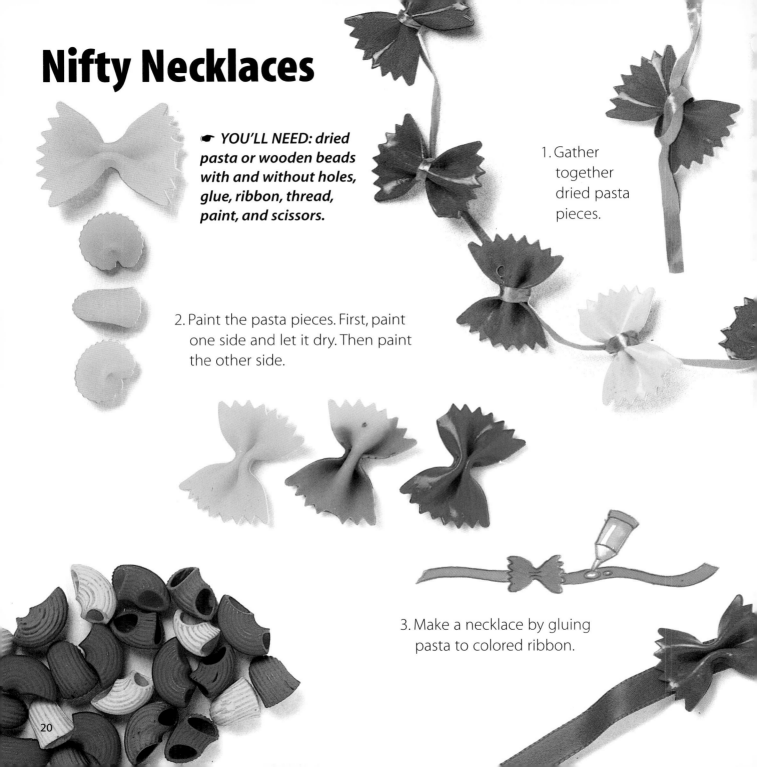

☞ **YOU'LL NEED: dried pasta or wooden beads with and without holes, glue, ribbon, thread, paint, and scissors.**

1. Gather together dried pasta pieces.

2. Paint the pasta pieces. First, paint one side and let it dry. Then paint the other side.

3. Make a necklace by gluing pasta to colored ribbon.

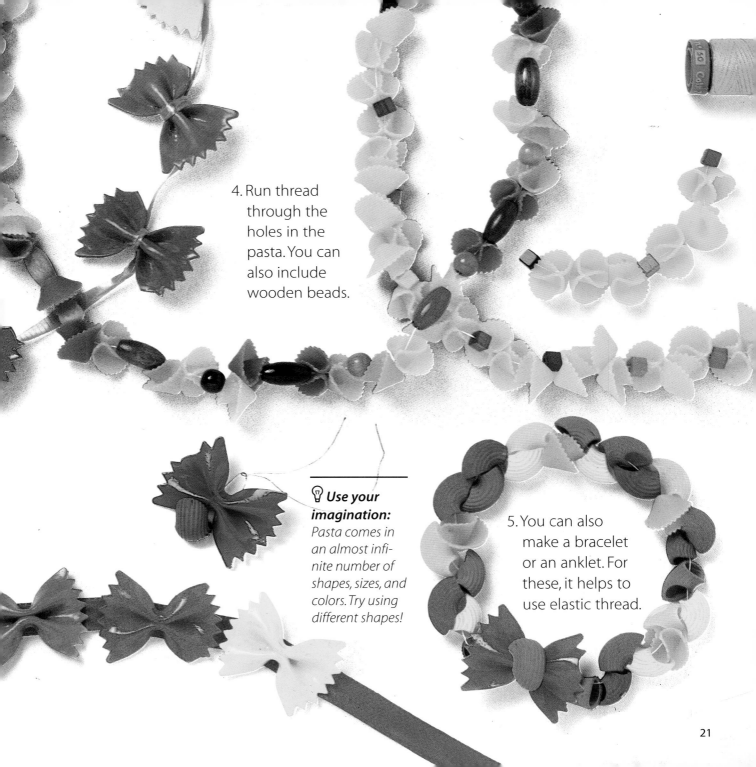

4. Run thread through the holes in the pasta. You can also include wooden beads.

💡 **Use your imagination:** *Pasta comes in an almost infinite number of shapes, sizes, and colors. Try using different shapes!*

5. You can also make a bracelet or an anklet. For these, it helps to use elastic thread.

Way-Out Hippie Hair

☞ YOU'LL NEED: *glue, colored paper, metallic paper, tissue paper, pencil, glitter or sequins, markers, ribbon, and scissors.*

1. Cut narrow strips of tissue paper.

2. Cut two strips of metallic paper to fit around your head.

3. Make small, horizontal slits in the middle of one of the metallic strips. Run the narrow strips through the end slits. Leave the center free of strips.

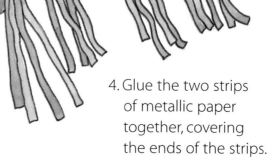

4. Glue the two strips of metallic paper together, covering the ends of the strips.

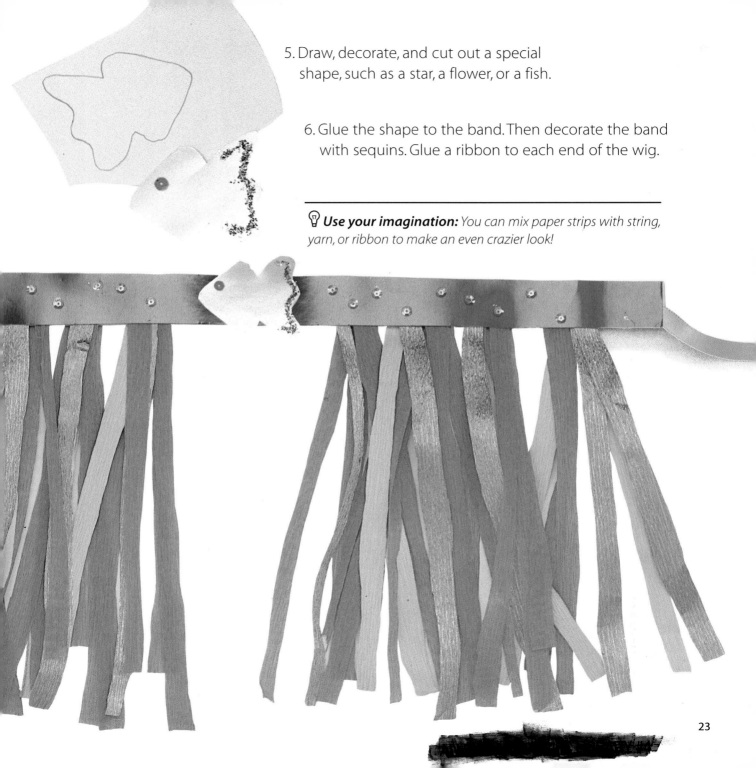

5. Draw, decorate, and cut out a special shape, such as a star, a flower, or a fish.

6. Glue the shape to the band. Then decorate the band with sequins. Glue a ribbon to each end of the wig.

💡 *Use your imagination:* *You can mix paper strips with string, yarn, or ribbon to make an even crazier look!*

A Native American Costume

☞ **YOU'LL NEED: colored construction paper, crepe paper, scissors, toothpicks, ribbon, and glue.**

1. Place the colored paper sheets one on top of the other.

2. For the shirt, fold a length of crepe paper in half.

3. Fold the crepe paper again a second time, as shown. Cut it to form sleeves.

4. For the headdress, cut a strip of construction paper. Glue a ribbon to each end.

5. Add feathers made of paper. Secure with a toothpick.

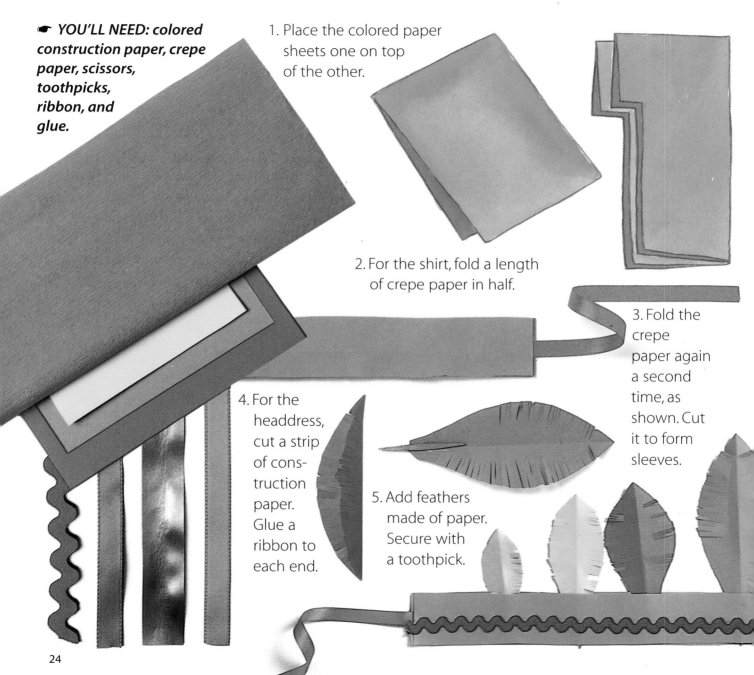

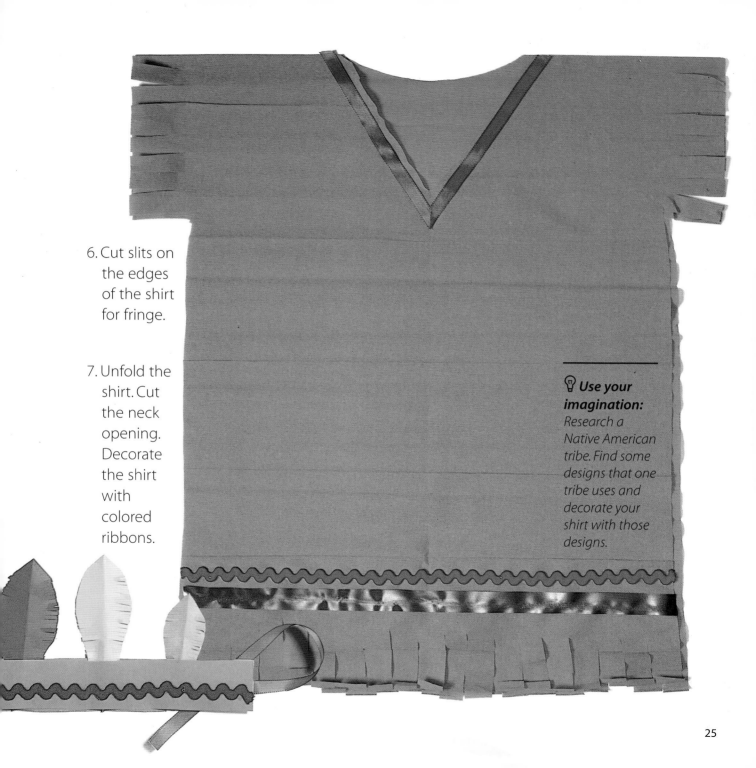

6. Cut slits on the edges of the shirt for fringe.

7. Unfold the shirt. Cut the neck opening. Decorate the shirt with colored ribbons.

💡 Use your imagination: *Research a Native American tribe. Find some designs that one tribe uses and decorate your shirt with those designs.*

A Magical Mask

☞ **YOU'LL NEED:**
*construction paper,
newspaper, a marker,
paper plates, paint, a
paintbrush, glue, and
scissors.*

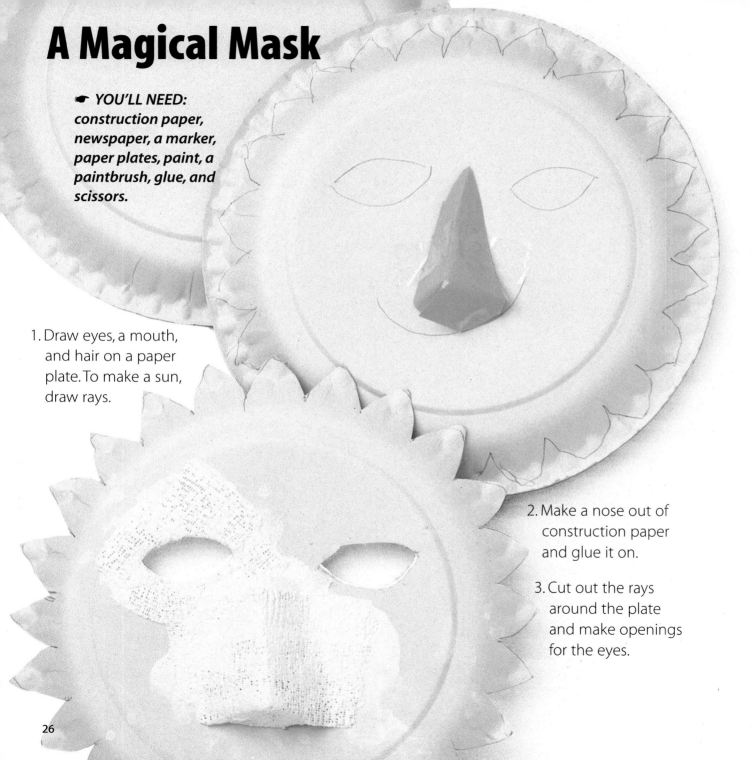

1. Draw eyes, a mouth,
   and hair on a paper
   plate. To make a sun,
   draw rays.

2. Make a nose out of
   construction paper
   and glue it on.

3. Cut out the rays
   around the plate
   and make openings
   for the eyes.

26

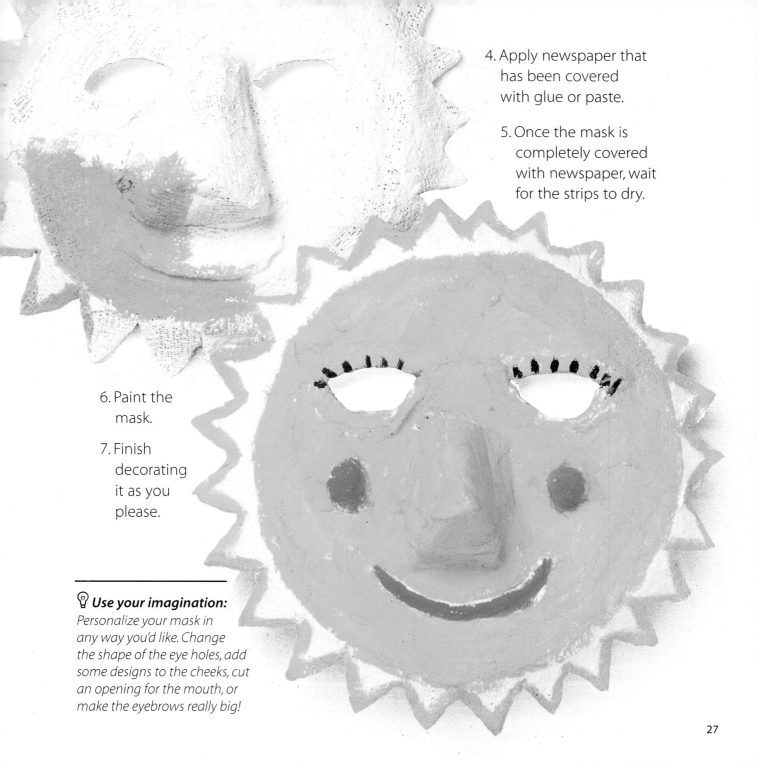

4. Apply newspaper that has been covered with glue or paste.

5. Once the mask is completely covered with newspaper, wait for the strips to dry.

6. Paint the mask.

7. Finish decorating it as you please.

💡 **Use your imagination:**
Personalize your mask in any way you'd like. Change the shape of the eye holes, add some designs to the cheeks, cut an opening for the mouth, or make the eyebrows really big!

Perfect Paradise Jewelry

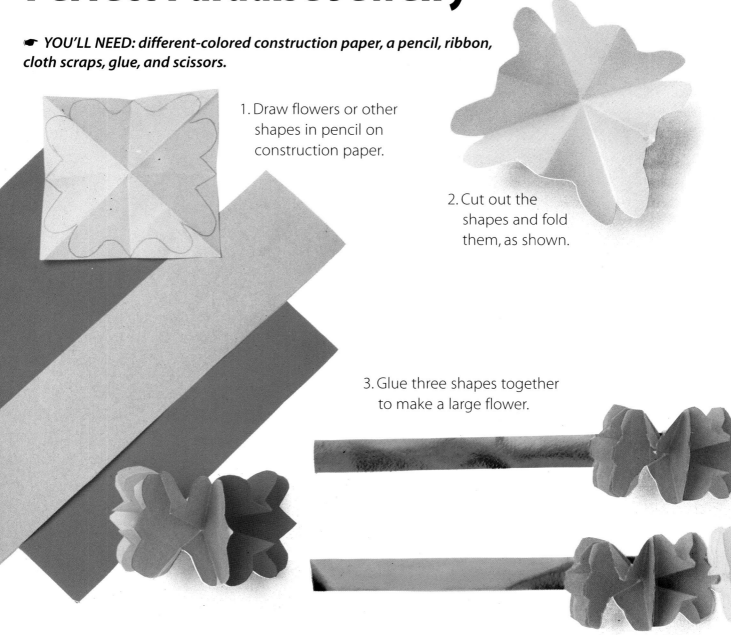

☛ **YOU'LL NEED:** *different-colored construction paper, a pencil, ribbon, cloth scraps, glue, and scissors.*

1. Draw flowers or other shapes in pencil on construction paper.

2. Cut out the shapes and fold them, as shown.

3. Glue three shapes together to make a large flower.

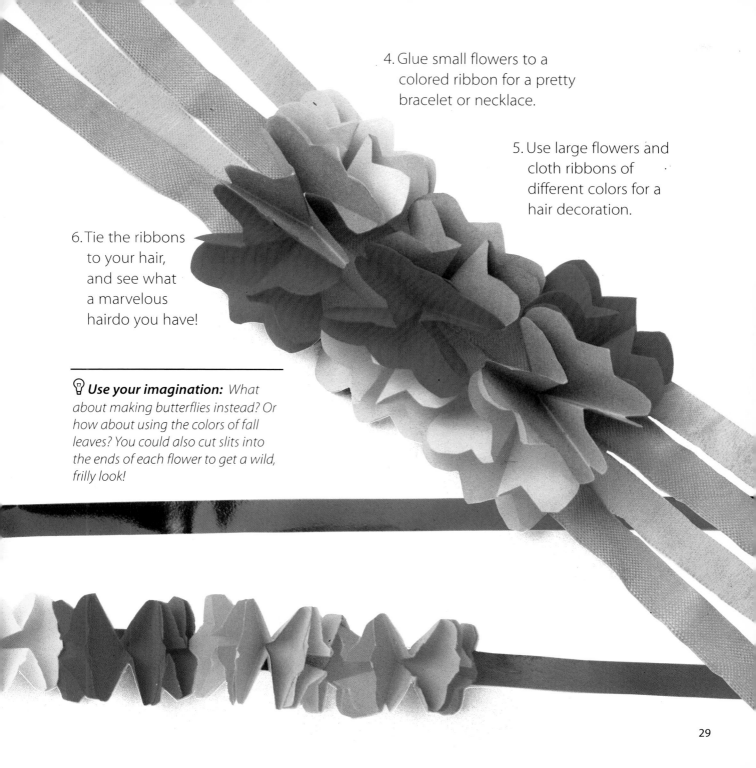

4. Glue small flowers to a colored ribbon for a pretty bracelet or necklace.

5. Use large flowers and cloth ribbons of different colors for a hair decoration.

6. Tie the ribbons to your hair, and see what a marvelous hairdo you have!

💡 *Use your imagination: What about making butterflies instead? Or how about using the colors of fall leaves? You could also cut slits into the ends of each flower to get a wild, frilly look!*

WHERE TO GET SUPPLIES

Art & Woodcrafters Supply, Inc.

www.artwoodcrafter.com

Order a catalog or browse online for many different craft supplies.

Craft Supplies

www.craftsfaironline.com/Supplies.html

This online craft store features many different sites, each featuring products for specific hobbies.

Darice, Inc.

21160 Drake Road

Strongsville, OH 44136-6699

www.darice.com

Order a catalog or browse online for many different craft supplies.

Making Friends

www.makingfriends.com

Offers many kits and products for children's crafts.

National Artcraft

7996 Darrow Road

Twinsburg, OH 44087

www.nationalartcraft.com

This craft store features many products available through its catalog or online.

FOR MORE INFORMATION

Books

Chapman, Gillian. *Art From Fabric: With Projects Using Rags, Old Clothes, and Remnants.* New York, NY: Thomson Learning, 1995.

Chapman, Gillian. *Autumn* (Seasonal Crafts). Chatham, NJ: Raintree/Steck Vaughn, 1997.

Connor, Nikki. *Cardboard Boxes* (Creating Crafts From). Providence, RI: Copper Beech Books, 1996.

Gordon, Lynn. *52 Great Art Projects For Kids.* San Francisco, CA: Chronicle Books, 1996.

King, Penny. *Animals* (Artists' Workshop). New York, NY: Crabtree Publishing, 1996.

Newby, Nicole. *Cool Clay.* Mahwah, NJ: Troll, 1996.

Ross, Kathy. *The Best Holiday Crafts Ever.* Brookfield, CT: Millbrook Publishing, 1996.

Smith, Alistair. *Big Book of Papercraft.* Newton, MA: Educational Development Center, 1996.

Video

Blue's Clues Arts & Crafts. Nickelodeon. (1998).

Web Sites

Crafts For Kids

www.craftsforkids.miningco.com/ mbody.htm

Many different arts and crafts activities are explained in detail.

Family Crafts

www.family.go.com

Search for crafts by age group. Projects include instructions, supply list, and helpful tips.

KinderCrafts

www.EnchantedLearning.com/Crafts

Step-by-step instructions explain how to make animal, dinosaur, box, and paper crafts, plus much more.

Making Friends

www.makingfriends.com

Contains hundreds of craft ideas with detailed instructions for children ages 2 to 12, including paper dolls, summer crafts, yucky stuff, and holiday crafts.

INDEX